Maths
made easy

Preschool
ages 3-5
Adding and Taking Away

Author and Consultant
Su Hurrell

DK

LONDON • NEW YORK • MUNICH • MELBOURNE • DELHI

More than

Look ✔ the necklace with more beads

✔

Look ✔ the tower with more bricks

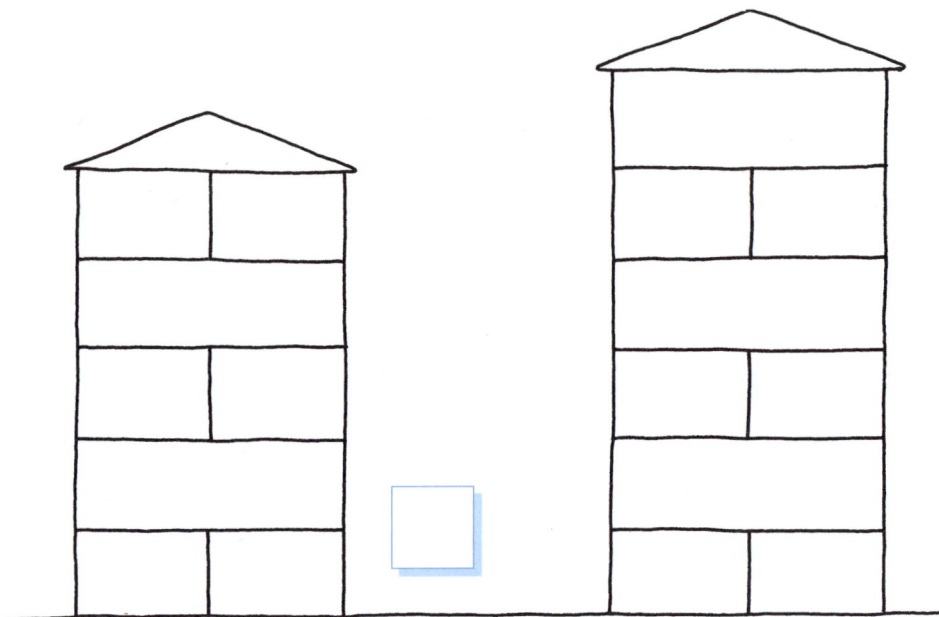

Look ✔ the ladybird with more spots

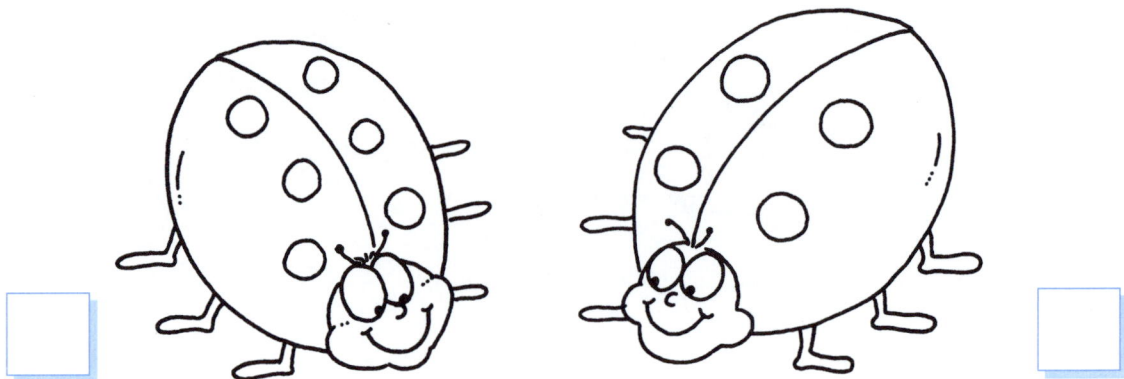

0 1 2 3 4 5 6 7 8 9 10

More than

Draw more beads

Draw more bricks

Draw more spots

0 1 2 3 4 5 6 7 8 9 10

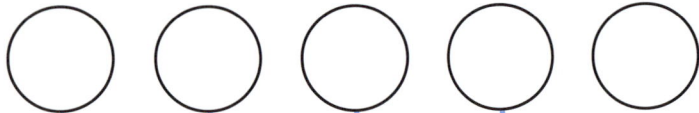

1 more than

Match the circles   ✔ 1 more

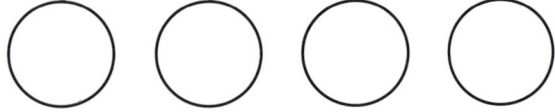

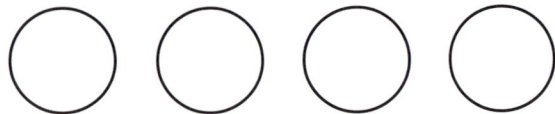

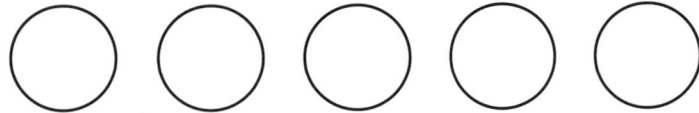

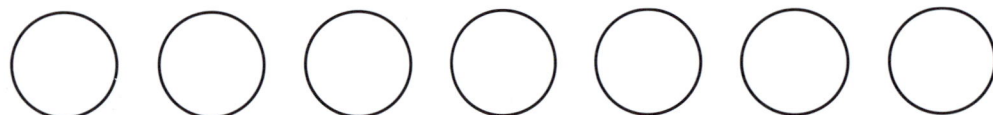

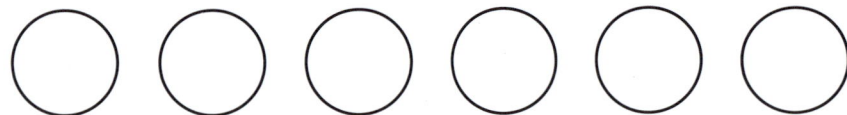

Count how many

  and 1 more  makes

 and 1 more  makes

0 1 2 3 4 5 6 7 8 9 10

4

And 1 more

Draw 1 more   Count how many

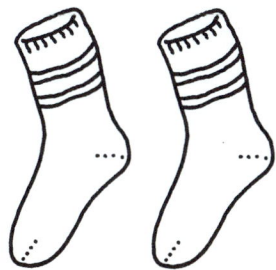 and   makes

 and   makes

 and   makes

And 1 more

3 and 1 more makes

4 and 1 more makes

1 and 1 more makes

2 and 1 more makes

0 1 2 3 4 5 6 7 8 9 10

2 more than

Match the hats   ✔ 2 more

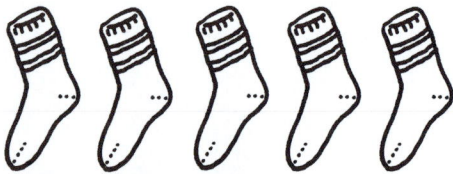
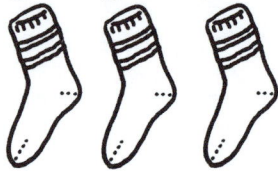

Count how many

 and 2 more  makes

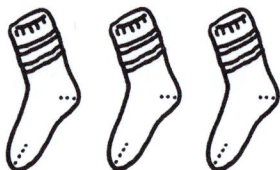 and 2 more 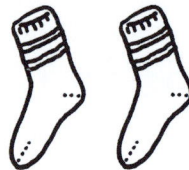 makes

0 1 2 3 4 5 6 7 8 9 10

And 2 more

Draw 2 more   Count how many

 and   makes ☐

 and   makes ☐

 and   makes ☐

 and   makes ☐

And 2 more

1 and 2 more makes ☐   2 and 2 more makes ☐

4 and 2 more makes ☐   3 and 2 more makes ☐

0 1 2 3 4 5 6 7 8 9 10

3 more than

Match the cakes ✔ 3 more

☐

☐

☐

☐

☐

☐

Count how many

 and 3 more  makes ☐

 and 3 more  makes ☐

0 1 2 3 4 5 6 7 8 9 10

☆

And 3 more

Draw 3 more — Count how many

 and makes ☐

 and makes ☐

 and makes ☐

 and makes ☐

And 3 more

3 and 3 more makes ☐

1 and 3 more makes ☐

4 and 3 more makes ☐

2 and 3 more makes ☐

0 1 2 3 4 5 6 7 8 9 10

4 more than

Match the buttons   ✔ 4 more

Count how many

and 4 more   makes

and 4 more   makes

0 1 2 3 4 5 6 7 8 9 10

And 4 more

Draw 4 more

Count how many

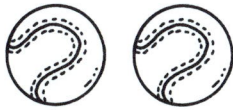 and   makes [ ]

 and   makes [ ]

 and   makes [ ]

 and   makes [ ]

And 4 more

4 and 4 more makes [ ]

1 and 4 more makes [ ]

2 and 4 more makes [ ]

3 and 4 more makes [ ]

0 1 2 3 4 5 6 7 8 9 10

5 more than

Count how many

 and 5 more   makes

 and 5 more   makes

0 1 2 3 4 5 6 7 8 9 10

And 5 more

Draw 5 more

Count how many

 and   makes ☐

 and   makes ☐

and   makes ☐

And 5 more

2 and 5 more makes ☐   3 and 5 more makes ☐

4 and 5 more makes ☐   5 and 5 more makes ☐

0 1 2 3 4 5 6 7 8 9 10

Count how many

○ and ○ ○ more makes ⬜

○ ○ and ○ ○ / ○ ○ more makes ⬜

○ ○ ○ and ○ more makes ⬜

○ ○ / ○ ○ / ○ ○ and ○ ○ ○ more makes ⬜

○ ○ ○ / ○ ○ / ○ ○ and ○ ○ more makes ⬜

○ ○ ○ and ○ ○ ○ more makes ⬜

○ ○ and ○ ○ more makes ⬜

○ ○ / ○ ○ / ○ ○ and ○ ○ / ○ ○ / ○ ○ more makes ⬜

○ ○ ○ and ○ ○ ○ / ○ ○ more makes ⬜

0 1 2 3 4 5 6 7 8 9 10

Count how many

1 and 1 more makes ☐

3 and 1 more makes ☐

3 and 2 more makes ☐

1 and 3 more makes ☐

2 and 1 more makes ☐

3 and 4 more makes ☐

2 and 5 more makes ☐

4 and 3 more makes ☐

2 and 3 more makes ☐

5 and 5 more makes ☐

4 and 4 more makes ☐

4 and 5 more makes ☐

3 and 5 more makes ☐

3 and 3 more makes ☐

0 1 2 3 4 5 6 7 8 9 10

Fewer than

Look ✔ the tree with fewer apples

Look ✔ the plate with fewer cakes

Look ✔ the dog with fewer spots

16

Notes for parents

This book is designed for children who have the ability to count from zero up to 20, with a good understanding of the order and value of numbers. If your child has these skills they are probably ready to explore and investigate problem solving using numbers.

Content

By working through this book your child will discover the fun of adding numbers together and taking them away. Your child will learn:

- the concept of *more than*, initially by looking and then by counting;
- the concept of adding numbers together;
- the language involved in the addition process;
- the symbols of addition;
- the concept of *less than*, *fewer than*, initially by looking and then by counting;
- the concept of subtraction;
- the language involved in the subtraction process;
- the symbols used in subtraction;
- the use of the symbols of both addition and subtraction to complete sums.

How to help your child

A child learns through hands-on experiences so it is important that your child has had a range of practical experiences before attempting the activities in the book.

You can offer these experiences of adding and taking away using everyday familiar objects. Your child may need counters, buttons, or similar small objects to help them work through the book. As they become confident and familiar with the activities, the drawn objects may be sufficient. But have something available just in case!

This book should be an enjoyable experience for both you and your child, a shared time together. So make sure that your child is alert and not too tired. Keep the time spent appropriate to the age and level of concentration of your child.

Build your child's confidence by praise and encouragement. Celebrate their success.

In most of the activities your child will be asked to fill in the missing numbers, so watch for reversals and make sure the child begins writing the number at the top. Your child can refer to the number line at any time.

The pages are designed for your child to colour, which develops pencil control, eye and hand co-ordination, and builds up concentration. So make sure there is a range of coloured pencils or felt-tip pens available. Crayons are usually too thick for such activities.

For writing and drawing your child will need a sharp, soft pencil. If the pencil is too hard, they will have difficulty seeing their work and this will lead to frustration.

There are similar activities throughout, but the book becomes more challenging as it progresses. The progression is gradual, beginning by adding one more, then two more, up to five more. The same is true for subtracting; first taking one away, then two, up to five.

After each stage there are two revision pages.

The final three pages introduce the symbols and their positions within problems, or sums.

Words are used throughout the book so the child may need help with reading.

Talk about the activities on each page and make sure your child understands what they are to do.

Try and present the activities as problems when talking about them, as this will give your child a sense of using these number operations for a purpose. Without this practical application your child will see sums as meaningless tasks with no relevance to their lives. If this happens they will not be able to make full use of their understanding and skills later.

Remember this book is for fun as well as being educational, so stop before your child loses concentration or is restless. This will ensure they want to come back for more!

Vocabulary used in the book

more than	general statement to indicate that there is more in that set or group than in this one
1 (2, 3, 4, 5) more than	to show how many more in a particular set
and 1 (2, 3, 4, 5) more	is the beginning of adding on more to a quantity of numbers
makes	is used instead of the symbol = For example, 3 and 1 more makes 4
fewer than	as a mathematical term this describes the difference between two numbers
1 (2, 3, 4, 5) fewer	this describes how many fewer in a set. (The word less may be used by the child at the early stages of beginning to understand number operations. It should be used when describing quantities rather than numbers. So try and encourage your child to use "fewer", the right vocabulary, at the early stages as it will be less confusing for them when they go to school.)
take 1 (2, 3, 4, 5) away	this describes the physical process children use to make some sets have fewer in them
left	this is used at the end of a taking away process to enable the child to understand that the number remaining is what they now have left
symbols	are: + − and =
+	means "and"
−	means "take away"
=	means "makes"

How to use the book

You have to make sure that your child has had many practical experiences before starting each page.

Introduce your child to the vocabulary they are going to meet.

Number line

There is a number line up to 10 at the bottom of the pages. This will help the child to recall what the numbers look like. The number line can also be used to encourage your child to "count on".

Number line

Counting on and back

This can be introduced as a fun activity before starting the book. Create your own number line – it can go beyond 10. Encourage your child to count on using a hopping motion from number to number:

$$0 \quad 1 \quad 2 \quad 3 \quad 4 \quad 5 \quad 6 \quad 7 \quad 8 \quad 9 \quad 10$$

For example, for "4 and 2 more ..." put a finger on the number 4 and make the child do two jumps, first landing at 5 and then at 6, so that the answer is 6.

Subtraction is the same, counting the number of jumps backwards. Zero, or nothing, is introduced during the process of subtraction and is featured in the number line.

By progressing slowly through the book, exploring one number at a time, you can help your child to become familiar with the number combinations and help them with mental calculations.

Page-by-page notes

Pages 4, 6, 8, 10, and 12 – Match

The rows have been arranged horizontally to help your child work out how many more there are. Your child can match one object to another by drawing a line between the objects.

At the end of each row is a box. Your child should tick in the box at the end of the line that has "more" in it.

Count how many

Your child has to add on. For example, count how many 4 hats and 2 more hats makes.

Encourage your child to count on, starting at the 4 – then 5 then 6.

If children still need practical support such as counters and fingers, use them until children feel confident to manage without.

It is a good idea to introduce counting on with the number line. This will encourage your child to begin counting from the existing number instead of going back to number 1, which children frequently do.

Offer your child plenty of praise and encouragement.

Pages 5, 7, 9, 11, 13 – And 1 more

Draw 1 (2, 3, 4, 5) more

Your child has to draw one more of the object shown on the page, count how many there are altogether, and write the answer in the box.

Again, encourage your child to count on to reach the answer.

And 1 (2, 3, 4, 5) more

Here, numbers are introduced and replace the objects.

Allow your child to use counters or fingers if they are not confident without them. Build up their confidence so they are willing to try without the props!

Do make use of the number line to help your child with the addition.

Read out the words of the sums as this gives meaning to the operation.

If possible try and use these examples of adding numbers within the context of your child's daily life; when laying the table, handing out biscuits, etc.

Pages 14 and 15 – Revision

Page 14 is a page of sums, on which circles have been given to help with the addition.

Page 15 progresses to use numbers alone, without the help of objects or circles.

Pages 18, 20, 22, 24, 26 – 1 (2, 3, 4, 5) fewer than

Count how many, Tick 1 fewer

Your child has to tick the box under the group of objects that contains one fewer.

Initially use a variety of vocabulary to help your child understand the concept. For example, "what is the difference?", "1 fewer".

To begin with, your child may need counters in front of them to give them confidence but if you have been playing games using many practical examples this may not be necessary.

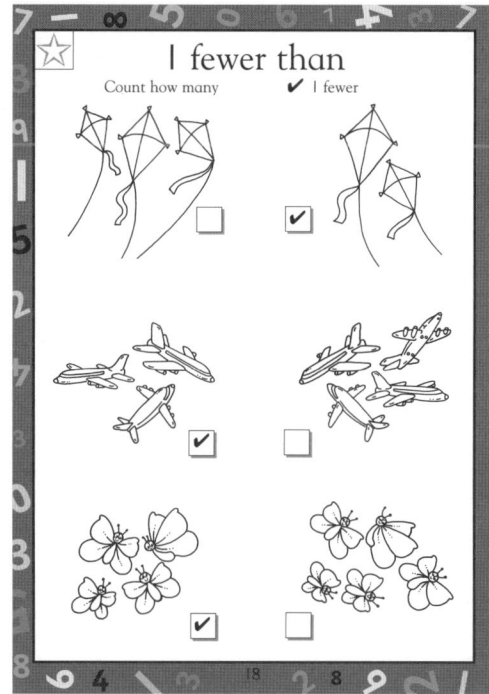

Pages 19, 21, 23, 25, 27 – Take 1 (2, 3, 4, 5) away

Cross 1 out, Count how many are left

Your child has to cross one of the objects out and then count how many remain.

The illustration is converted into a sum, so children can begin to see the connection between the practical and the abstract form of numbers.

Children should colour the page before crossing out the objects.

Pages 28 and 29 – Revision

Page 28 is a page of sums where your child crosses out 1 (or 2, 3, 4, 5) object(s) and writes the answer in the box.

Page 29 is the same process but without the objects. Until your child is confident they may like to use counters or their fingers.

The number line can support your child. Put a finger or a pencil on the first number and make one hop (or however many hops) backwards. The number you land on is the answer. Eventually your child should be able to try without props.

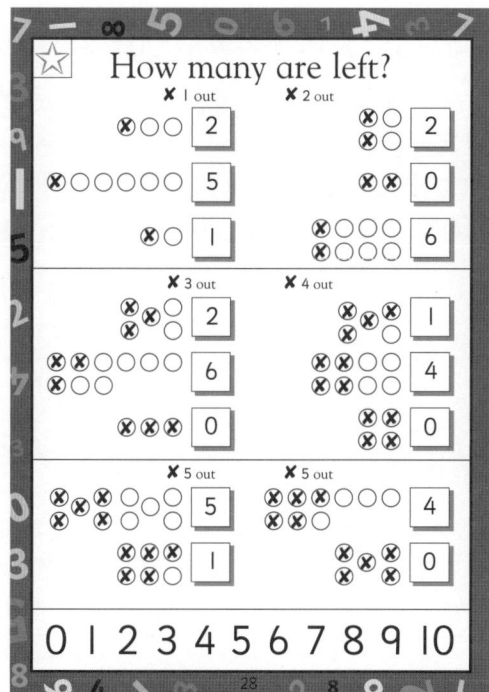

Some answers may be 0 (also nothing or zero). Play games with your child to introduce this concept: "There are two sweets and you eat two. How many are left?"

If the whole page is too daunting or confusing, cover the lower sums with a blank piece of paper. This will enable your child to concentrate on one sum at a time.

Page 30 – Special symbols
The addition sign and the equals sign are introduced.

Talk this through with your child, explaining that the signs are used instead of the words, but mean the same thing.

Page 31 – Special symbols
This page introduces the subtraction symbol and also uses the equals sign as before.

Your child has to complete the sums using the symbols instead of the words. Help your child initially by saying the words aloud.

Page 32 – Now you can do these sums
A page of sums including both addition and subtraction as well as sums without the symbols. This page introduces the task of putting the right symbol in the right place. Talk it through with your child encouraging them to choose the right symbol.

Special symbols

+ means **and**   = means **makes**

Count how many

○○ / ○	and	○ ○	makes	5
3	and	2	makes	5
3	+	2	=	5
○○	and	○	makes	3
2	and	1	makes	3
2	+	1	=	3
○○ / ○○	and	○ ○	makes	6
4	and	2	makes	6
4	+	2	=	6

0 1 2 3 4 5 6 7 8 9 10

30

Now you can do these sums

4 + 2 =	6		6 – 1 =	5
2 + 2 =	4		5 – 3 =	2
3 + 3 =	6		4 – 4 =	0
7 + 1 =	8		10 – 2 =	8
6 – 4 =	2		9 – 3 =	6
5 + 5 =	10		6 + 3 =	9
7 – 2 =	5		5 + 4 =	9
2 + 5 =	7		1 – 1 =	0

Write the symbol

| 3 + 1 = | 4 | | 3 – 2 = | 1 |
| 2 + 2 = | 4 | | 4 – 1 = | 3 |

0 1 2 3 4 5 6 7 8 9 10

32

Fewer than

Draw fewer sweets

Draw fewer pennies

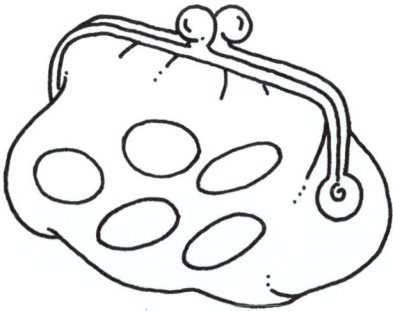

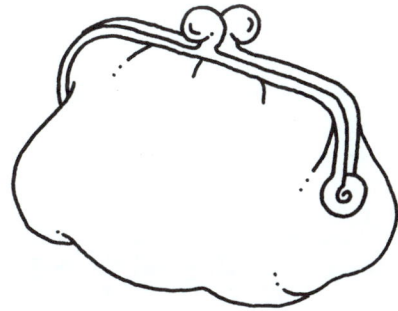

Draw fewer eggs

Draw fewer socks

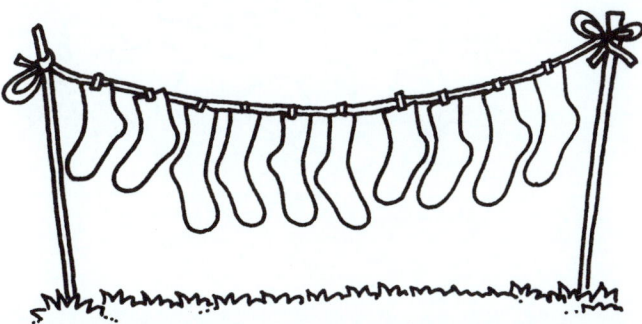

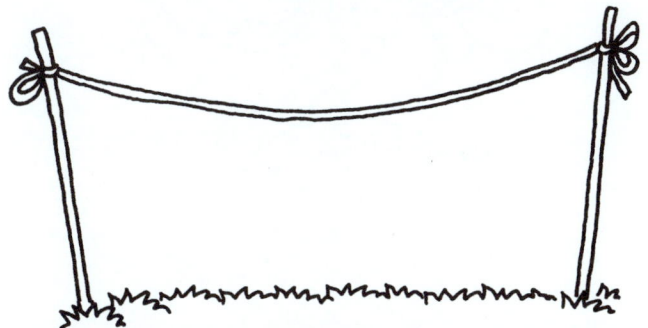

17

I fewer than

Count how many   ✔ I fewer

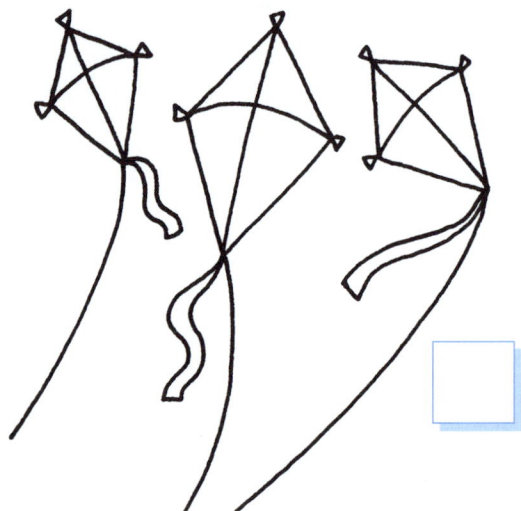

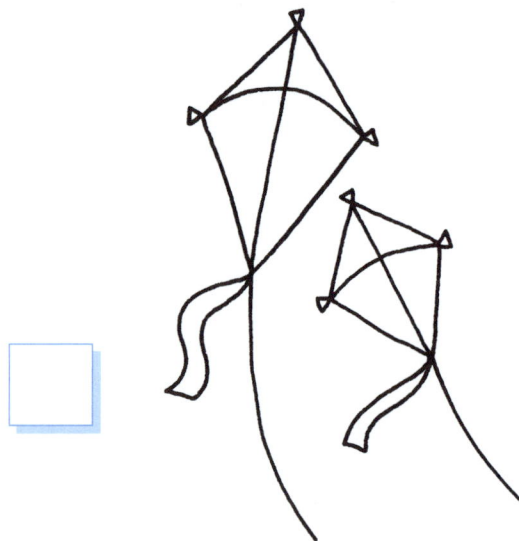

Take 1 away

✗ 1 out   Count how many are left

[ ] left

5 take away 1 makes [ ]

[ ] left

2 take away 1 makes [ ]

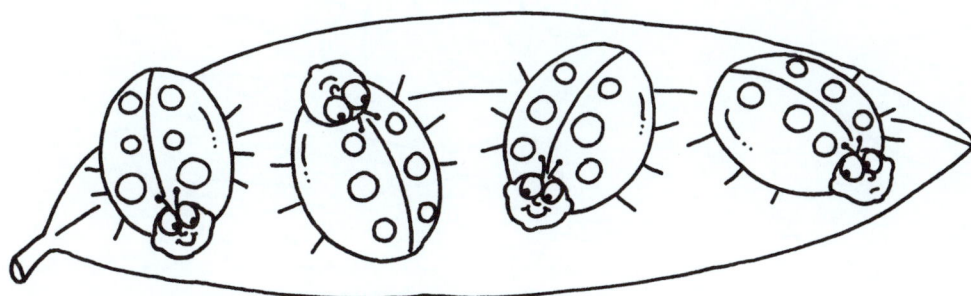

[ ] left

4 take away 1 makes [ ]

2 fewer than

Count how many   ✔ 2 fewer

☆

0 1 2 3 4 5 6 7 8 9 10

20

Take 2 away

Count how many are left

4 take away 2 makes ☐

5 take away 2 makes ☐

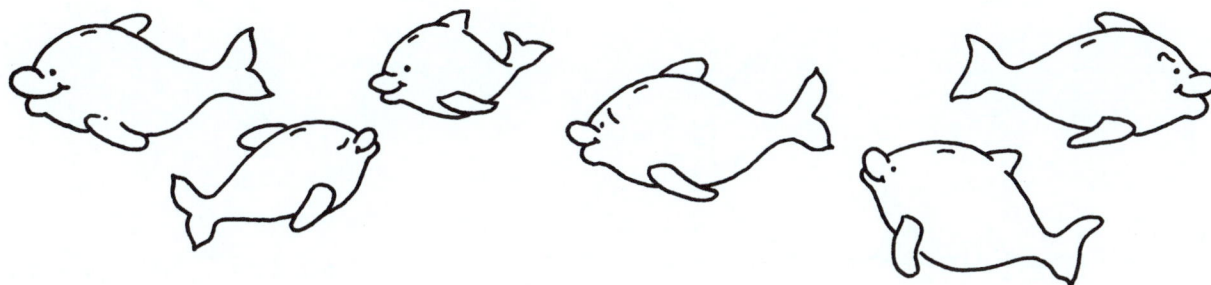

6 take away 2 makes ☐

0 1 2 3 4 5 6 7 8 9 10

3 fewer than

Count how many apples

Draw 3 fewer apples on this tree

Count how many apples

Draw 3 fewer apples on this tree

Count how many apples

0 1 2 3 4 5 6 7 8 9 10

Take 3 away

6 take away 3 makes ▢

5 take away 3 makes ▢

9 take away 3 makes ▢

0 1 2 3 4 5 6 7 8 9 10

4 fewer than

Count how many   ✔ 4 fewer

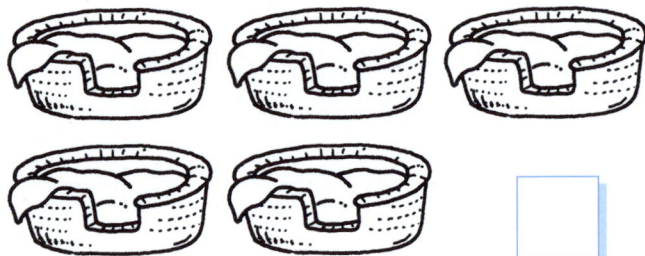

0 1 2 3 4 5 6 7 8 9 10

Take 4 away

Count how many are left

8 take away 4 makes [ ]

5 take away 4 makes [ ]

4 take away 4 makes [ ]

0 1 2 3 4 5 6 7 8 9 10

25

5 fewer than

Count how many   ✔ 5 fewer

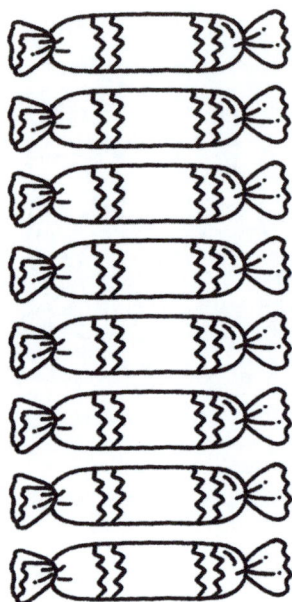

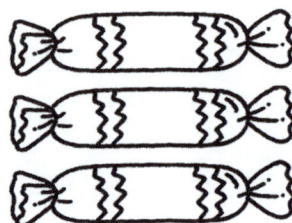

0 1 2 3 4 5 6 7 8 9 10

Take 5 away

✗ 5 out   Count how many are left

9 take away 5 makes [ ]

7 take away 5 makes [ ]

5 take away 5 makes [ ]

0 1 2 3 4 5 6 7 8 9 10

27

How many are left?

✗ 1 out

○ ○ ○ ☐

○ ○ ○ ○ ○ ○ ☐

○ ○ ☐

✗ 2 out

○ ○
○ ○ ☐

○ ○ ☐

○ ○ ○ ○
○ ○ ○ ○ ☐

✗ 3 out

○ ○ ○
○ ○ ☐

○ ○ ○ ○ ○ ○
○ ○ ○ ☐

○ ○ ○ ☐

✗ 4 out

○ ○ ○
○ ○ ☐

○ ○ ○ ○
○ ○ ○ ○ ☐

○ ○
○ ○ ☐

✗ 5 out

○ ○ ○ ○ ○
○ ○ ○ ○ ☐

○ ○ ○
○ ○ ○ ☐

✗ 5 out

○ ○ ○ ○ ○
○ ○ ○ ☐

○ ○
○ ○ ○ ☐

0 1 2 3 4 5 6 7 8 9 10

Take away

3 take away 2 makes ☐

4 take away 1 makes ☐

6 take away 2 makes ☐

5 take away 3 makes ☐

10 take away 1 makes ☐

7 take away 5 makes ☐

3 take away 3 makes ☐

8 take away 2 makes ☐

9 take away 1 makes ☐

6 take away 5 makes ☐

4 take away 4 makes ☐

7 take away 2 makes ☐

8 take away 4 makes ☐

10 take away 2 makes ☐

0 1 2 3 4 5 6 7 8 9 10

Special symbols

+ means **and**   = means **makes**

Count how many

○○○ ○   and   ○○   makes   ☐

3   and   2   makes   ☐

3   +   2   =   ☐

○○   and   ○   makes   ☐

2   and | makes   ☐

2   + | =   ☐

○○○○   and   ○○   makes   ☐

4   and   2   makes   ☐

4   +   2   =   ☐

0 1 2 3 4 5 6 7 8 9 10

Special symbols

— means **take away**   = means **makes**

Count how many

6   take away   1   makes   [ ]

6   –   1   =   [ ]

4   take away   2   makes   [ ]

4   –   2   =   [ ]

5   take away   3   makes   [ ]

5   –   3   =   [ ]

0 1 2 3 4 5 6 7 8 9 10

⭐ Now you can do these sums

4 + 2 = ⬜

2 + 2 = ⬜

3 + 3 = ⬜

7 + 1 = ⬜

6 – 1 = ⬜

5 – 3 = ⬜

4 – 4 = ⬜

10 – 2 = ⬜

---

6 – 4 = ⬜

5 + 5 = ⬜

7 – 2 = ⬜

2 + 5 = ⬜

9 – 3 = ⬜

6 + 3 = ⬜

5 + 4 = ⬜

1 – 1 = ⬜

Write the symbol

3 ⬜ 1 = 4

2 ⬜ 2 = 4

3 ⬜ 2 = 1

4 ⬜ 1 = 3

0 1 2 3 4 5 6 7 8 9 10